Happy Heifer

**A memoir of a girl, her dad,
and the cows that bound them together**

**Written By
Becke' Martens Stuart**

For you, Dad.
Simply because you asked.

Prologue

"We were together. I forget the rest."
Walt Whitman

"Hop out, Lulu. I'm gonna go put that cow down," Dad said. At the age of forty something, I was still jumping into the red Pioneer ATV to go check cows with my Dad. We covered a few pastures that cold February day and then came upon an older cow who had gone down while in labor. We tried every trick in the book to get that cow up. We even put a rope around her neck and pulled her with the Pioneer to get her going. The poor mama didn't budge. The calf had died inside of her. Dad knew it was a lost cause. The cow was too old to try to save. It takes wisdom to know whether to call a vet or cut your losses.

We drove back to the house so Dad could get his shotgun. "Hop out, Lulu," he said. Out of respect, I normally listened, but this time, I held my ground.

"No, Dad, I'm going with you," I said. "I can handle it." I stared him down until he realized I wasn't going anywhere.

The Pioneer chugged its way up the steep hill, my heartbeat matching each rev of the engine. Sweet old momma still hadn't moved. Her pain was displayed in each fleck of her eyes. Dad made me turn my eyes away, trying to shield me from sights one couldn't unsee. He was being merciful not just to the cow, but to me. One single "POP" washed away all of her pain.

I didn't cry. I had learned too much over the years. But I did ponder why I had been so eager to go with my Dad to end her life.

3

Death is hard enough when shared but just about intolerable when left to yourself. I wanted to share the grief with him and carry as much of it as I could.

Sharing cows was our thing...in the good times and the bad.

Beginnings
"Tell me, what is it you plan to do
with your one wild and precious life?"
Mary Oliver

A lot of water has run under the bridge of
my childhood days. 3950 Bridgewater Lane housed
the first of my memories. Overlooking a few
wooded acres and a creek sat the home Dad built
for our family. We drove on that bridge every time
we returned from town; it was the secret portal to
my childhood. After the bridge, we turned by our
mailbox that rose from a patch of marigolds and
onto our circular gravel driveway. Cows and
barbed wire fence lined each side of the pathway
leading us to our brick home, shop, and red gate
that further led to our barn, pond, and five acres.
 The shop was Dad's territory. It sat atop a
small mound where White Lightning, his 78' Chevy
truck, was always parked. Even though the shop
felt huge to my little eyes, it was safe. There was
something reassuring about watching Dad work
that brought me comfort. The unforgiving
sawblades, explosive water sprayers, and power
drills didn't unnerve me, but created a sense of
trust in my Dad. I figured if he could handle these
beasts, then he must have the rest of the world
under control as well.
 Big heaters tucked away in the upper corner
recesses of the shop glowed red in the winter
time. They kept Dad warm when he had to play
Santa Claus and put together little red wagons the
night before Christmas. The giant hands that built
homes, shops, churches, businesses, and red
wagons were the same hands that held me in the

recliner and wrestled with me on our brown, shaggy carpet.

Dad's office was nestled inside the right corner of the shop where his current blueprints lay sprawled across his giant desk. A sticky fly catcher dangled from the ceiling that called me to take a peek at guts and dying flights.

Just past the red gate that separated yard from pasture was the pond. The pond held little significance to me because there were no fish in it. It provided water for the cattle and looked pretty enough—in a murky pond kind of way--and that was about it. One day that all changed. Dad decided we didn't need the pond anymore, so he hopped onto his backhoe and started digging large trenches so the pond would drain.

My first panic attack happened right then and there. The so-called, non-existent fish were flopping three feet in every direction. My heart started pounding to the cadence of "save-the-fish." Mason jars and buckets in tow, my friend Amy, older brother Devin, and I plopped ourselves right into the muck and mire. The mud came all the way up to my cut off jean shorts, suctioned my legs like a sucker fish on a fish tank, and threatened to hold me hostage forever. Nevertheless, we persevered. No fish could be left behind. Not on my watch.

We dumped what we could into the creek. I housed the leftover tadpoles in water filled Mason jars with punctured lids. The next day, I took the jars to school and begged every other fourth grader to take one home. Most of them obliged and I can only imagine the string of cuss words that fell out of the mouths of parents during the 3 o'clock pick up line when their sons and daughters climbed into the back seats with their new little tailed friends.

Mrs. Whitlatch, a fifth-grade teacher close by, took the remainder of my orphaned tadpoles and dumped them into her large aquarium. Her beady eyes magnified by strong lenses had always scared me in the past, but it was in that moment that I realized appearances can be deceiving. Thanks to her glasses and kind soul, she saw a girl in need of every bit of compassion I was trying to offer to those swimmers. She rescued me that day when she supplied a haven for my future frogs.

Home was more than the four walls of a house. It was the front porch where I drew chalk lines and played hopscotch. It was the camper trailer where my best friend and I had sleepovers. It was the backside of my first horse, Buddy.

The front porch quickly became my play area. I chalked large hopscotch squares onto the concrete slab and jumped my way across. I built forts and sat with every single doll I owned, making sure each was well fed and groomed. I mothered a plethora of dolls, from China to Barbie, but Cody was my favorite. He had bright blue eyes and hair the color of sunshine. He smelled delicious, like a freshly bathed baby. The doll maker even gave him fake boy parts. *Gasp!* I was equally intrigued and equally horrified every time Cody needed a diaper change. God must have thrown back His head and laughed at me, knowing He would one day give me four *real* boys, each with very *real* boy parts, who would need a billion *real* diaper changes.

In the middle of our five acres sat an old camper. It must have been Amy's idea to sleep there one night. She was the adventurous one. It was quite the distance from the house, at least for a couple of nine-year old girls carrying their pillows in the pitch black. We settled ourselves in the bed and started talking about whose older sibling was more ridiculous.

"What's that sound?" Amy asked.

"I've never heard that it my life. Grab your stuff; we are making a run for it," I answered.

It was a black panther; we just knew it. As soon as we started running, we heard the panther again. It was so terrifying that we knew we would never make it back to the house without getting mauled, so we turned around and ran back to the safety of the camper. We lay there shaking and holding onto each other. When we pulled back the curtain to see if the coast was clear, a pair of glowing cow eyes stared back at us. We screamed the ceiling right off the camper, but no one came to our rescue. It wasn't bravery that convinced us to finish the night in the camper, but fear our parents would never let us do anything adventurous again. We willed ourselves to stay for the sake of future independence.

It was a wise choice, because now that we were in the double digits, we had big plans for horseback riding, the kind that didn't involve parents or pesky older siblings. I mounted Joe the Bay, and she sat atop Betsy the White. We were queens and pioneers and cowgirls, wrapped into two pre-adolescent bodies thirsting for one glorious swig of freedom. We made it all the way to Gulley Road, about one and a half miles away. We stopped and visited her grandfather. I'm not sure if we were more motivated by letting the horses rest and get a drink or grabbing some of his cookies for our own bellies. The dirt road held our deep secrets that day. We pushed Joe and Betsy too hard, but we didn't realize it until they started limping on the way back. That day, I discovered I liked the thrill of a quest, but nothing is as beautiful as the sight of home.

My girlhood was the smell of honeysuckle. I turned on the attic fan, opened the kitchen window, and breathed in the aroma as I helped in the kitchen. The kitchen sink is probably where we were first trained to work. My older brother, Devin, and I had to unload the dishes, load the dishes, hand wash all the other dishes, scrub potatoes, and fix tea. After the dishes were done, we doused Comet all over the yellow sink and scrubbed away the black marks the dishes left behind. Later, we rewarded ourselves by walking down to the honeysuckle bush. We plucked flowers, removed the green bud, and sucked the juice as if it were the very nectar of God Himself.

My girlhood was also the smell of the garden hose. Devin and I climbed mountains of gravel, rescued fish from the failing pond, and built forts in the rainstorms. Our five acres was our playground and the garden hose, our source of hydration.

Most of all, my girlhood was the smell of manure. Our land was a menagerie of every species of animal, an ark of our own making. If the horses, donkeys, cows, goats, rabbits, parakeets, gerbils, hamsters, fish, dogs, and cats didn't produce enough dung, then there was the annual spreading of chicken fertilizer on the pasture.

God's wonders were all around, each one wooing me towards His love. He was in the light of the lightning bugs at dusk, an assurance that He would light my path no matter how dark the night. He was in the cool creek, refreshment on the hottest of days and later, living water for my soul. He was in the newborn calf being born, teaching me that He is the author of all life.

But God knew I would need something else. God knew I would need something to bond me together with my Dad. It was early on when my lack of athletic ability surfaced. The fact that I was nicknamed Lulu at the age of two is my first clue. My Uncle Karl, missing half a finger, was hammering away alongside my Dad on wooden beams, the pillars and makings of our home on Bridgewater Lane that would cradle our family. I was toddling around, pigtails and dimpled thighs, making up my own words and tripping over toolboxes with ungracious tact. Karl said, "You know, Jerry, she looks like a little Lulu." My Dad never turned back. I was his Lulu from then on. Sure, I was also Becke', Honey Pie, and Sugar, but only Dad could call me Lulu and get away with it.

Instead of athletic ability, my vocal talents were rising like a bird on the heights, but my Dad couldn't appreciate it since he was tone deaf and all. Showing cattle would be the answer to making sure our hearts stayed bound, like twine on a bale of hay.

The fact that we even got into showing cattle must have been a victory cry that escaped from my father's wired-shut mouth. The year I started showing was the year Dad thought he was invincible. Dad untied one of Uncle Karl's heifers and she immediately threw a fit, knocked him down, kicked his head, and pinned it against the ground. Dad found himself in a bloodbath with bones poking in and out of his mouth and a jaw that had to be held in place. Mom, very pregnant with Schuyler Amelia, drove him 80 miles an hour to the hospital only to find that the computers were down. As Dad went through several blood-soaked towels, the hospital staff took their sweet time in admitting him.

I came home from a lake day with my friend, Whitney, only to find Granny and Pops at my house, announcing the awful news and keeping my siblings, Devin, Kiley, and Kirby, in line. I not only was terrified but felt horribly guilty for spending the day on the lake while my Dad was bleeding out.

Dad came home with a jaw that had been wired shut. It remained that way for eight whole weeks. Mom pureed cantaloupe and anything else she could figure out how to blend so Dad could suck it through a McDonald's milkshake straw. The doctor told Dad to keep a pair of pliers in his pocket to cut away the wires if he ever felt like he was going to vomit. The other option was to suffocate. This advice probably sounded over the top until we kids came down with the stomach bug. By the grace of God, those wires stayed on.

But a broken jaw didn't stop my Dad.

I remember the moment the idea of showing all began. I was eleven. We were at the Washington County Fair in Fayetteville, Arkansas, sitting on the bleachers taking in a cow show. I remember the yellow rod iron gate fencing that enclosed the ring and the feeling of being a very small fish in a very large pond. I didn't know the difference between a heifer (a female that hasn't had a calf) and a Hereford (a brand of beef cattle.)

Dad sat to my right and asked me if I'd be interested in doing what the kids leading cattle in the ring were doing. In all honesty, I had no idea what they were doing. But, for whatever reason, I said yes. My Dad grinned from Arkansas to Texas, squeezed my knee, and I knew in my heart it was the right answer.

I had no idea what I had gotten myself into. But I knew we would do it together, and that's all that mattered.

Dolly

"The beginning is the most important
part of the work."
Plato

Dolly was my first heifer. Dad had a passion
for the French breed of beef cattle called Limousin.
To my young brain, I couldn't conceive why they
had named a type of cow after the long black
vehicle that whisked people away to their high
school proms as well as gently carry off the dead to
their resting place. But, alas, we were to be
Limousin breeders and showers. Black or dark red,
preferably polled (born without horns), a gentle
disposition, and an excellent pedigree were
desirable traits. Hair that could grow and be
trained was a huge bonus; for show cattle, hair
covered a multitude of sins.

"Hello Dolly!" I'd say as I would attach the
white long rope to her thick blue halter. I'd wrap
the rope round and round my arm because I simply
didn't know any better. We would go round and
round the pasture, me in my bleached-out jeans
and winter pom pom hat and she in her pitiful
haircut that we were immensely proud of.

Dolly was perfect. We had absolutely no
idea what we were doing, and I doubt we won a
single show, but she was mine. Dolly was kind
enough to not drag me through the pasture or show
ring and humble enough to not care if she won. It
didn't seem to matter that my grey cowboy boots
were fake leather or that I wore my scotch comb
backwards in my back pocket facing out instead of
in. As with all things, a person has to start
somewhere. It was a pitiful start, but it was a start.
And I kept at it.

Some heifers were simply meant to be mommas. Dolly was one of them. There was love in her eyes, and they shone the brightest the moment she licked her first calf clean to help it start breathing. She had waited her whole life for that moment. Her motherly instinct took over as she nudged her calf to start moving, encouraging it to take its first wobbly steps towards the nourishment she could provide.

Dad

"Life's all about the right positive attitude.
There's a fine line between confidence and
arrogance."

Jerry Martens

My Dad was the baby of five children: the
baby by ten years. His parents and his only sister
took turns raising him, which allowed worn out
parents a break and Aunt Karleen lessons in
mothering. His light flax head of hair, dimples, and
oversized ears made him one endearing fella.
Having much older siblings helped shape who my
Dad became. He loved jokes, laughter, and being
an occasional pest. He was brave and fearless,
attempting anything and everything his much older
brothers tried. Weighing only a buck thirty-two, he
took up bull riding, where he not only stayed alive
but also stole the heart of the Rodeo Queen. For
life. He was charming, funny, a natural leader, and
wicked smart.

Dad was accepted at the University of
Arkansas, in hopes of going on to Louisiana State
University to become a veterinarian. Math was so
easy for him that he either did the equations in his
head or created his own methods for solving them.
Despite the correct answers, the college professors
wouldn't pass him because he didn't show his work.
Dad knew it was time to choose a different career
path.

Dad traded his dreams of being a vet for
being a builder. It was a wise choice since he
needed math on the fly and didn't have to prove his
correct answers. The beautiful, standing buildings
were all the proof that was needed. I have never
met a man more gifted at giving answers to

mathematical equations in his head than him. I only wish he had passed some of that genius down to me.

Dad's dreams of being a vet came true in another way. He did just about everything a vet could do with the medicines that were available to him. He restrained, delivered, vaccinated, tagged, hauled, separated, and examined his herd time and time again. He was confident in his abilities, and saved himself a ton of vet money in the process.

When he needed cows and heifers artificially inseminated, he called his buddy, Charlie Prentiss, who drove in from Oklahoma and charged a whopping ten bucks a head. Charlie was five-foot Santa Claus in the flesh, his sled a white mobile vet clinic. I loved peering into each compartment, taking in all of the medicines and instruments.

For deliveries, Dad only used a vet for one C-Section and a couple of other rare cases. All of the other times, he could get the job done with some calf pullers. One time, he delivered a calf while he had pneumonia and a raging fever. He was lying in a bed of snow, wondering if he was going to survive, but also fully aware that he was the calf's only hope of survival. He gave it one final pull, and the calf landed on top of him, which was all the warmth he needed in order to muster up the energy to make it back to the house. Perhaps they saved each other that day.

For pregnancy checks, Dad would often call a vet, as well. Pregnancy checks were necessary to know which of the herd was still open and needed to be bred. Rectal palpation was the cheapest and most convenient way to check for pregnancy. The vet would put on a palpation sleeve, which is a plastic glove that comes all the way up to the shoulder. After inserting his hand, the vet could feel the uterus, ovaries, and uterine arteries through the rectal wall.

One day during checks, Dad asked me if I wanted to check the mama for myself. "Heck yes!" I said. I pulled the lubricated plastic sleeve all the way up to my shoulder and tentatively stepped up to her manure encrusted backside. I knew I was about to invade her and certainly didn't want to harm her. I put my thumb and fingers together then slowly put my hand in and was taken back with how spacious and warm her insides were. No wonder Dad had to pull so many calves. If I were in that warm and cozy space, I wouldn't want to come out either.

I pushed my arm as far as it would go, my shoulder bumping against her rear. I felt around, but wasn't sure what I was supposed to be feeling, so I pulled my manure coated arm out and left the rest of the pregnancy checks to the professional.

My Dad was a life giver. Through five children, countless calves, homes for families, banks and car lots for jobs, churches for worship, and laughter for friends, he was always building places and spaces where lives could thrive.

Sweet 16

"Experience is the most brutal of teachers.
But you learn, my God, do you learn."
C. S. Lewis

One evening, when I was twelve, Dad came home from a cow sale and proceeded to unload his newest prized possession: a cow-calf pair. As I watched mama and baby girl exit the grey trailer, it was love at first sight. An obsession gripped my soul: I would be showing that little heifer. Doll Zula, the mom, was colored up like no cow I had ever laid eyes on. Her body and face were the color of a red sunset while her nose, eye area, and lashes were jet black. I swear, she got up every morning and put on her smoky eyeshadow. I approved of this regimen because makeup had recently become life to me, as well. Her daughter, Sweet 16, (named such because her sire--dad--held the name 16 Tons,) was the color of Cleopatra's hair. Her eyes were striking, almost too pretty for any bovine. She was a looker, and she knew it.

We nicknamed her Sweetie, but her name lied to us every single day. She was pompous and had quite the rebellious streak. While trying to halter break her, she did live up to the "16" part of her name as she acted like every other teenager in desperate need of escaping their parents.

I still hadn't learned that wrapping the rope around my arm while leading a cow might not be the safest course of action. It never seemed to be a big deal because Dolly never tried to get away. But Sweetie came along and bucked the system. She was Queen of the Nile and had no time for the lowly like me .

The first time she took off with me attached at the rope, the good Lord sent his angels down to keep me from imminent death. I face planted and was dragged through the pasture and back again. Through screams at her to stop, I choked down all manner of grass and manure. I can't believe my arm wasn't ripped out of its socket.

After that, I decided it might be time for a change in my halter breaking methods, since I wanted to see my 13th birthday and all. Instead of wrapping the halter rope around my arm, I wrapped it around and around my hand—between my thumb and index finger. This gave me some leverage but also hope that I would be able to let go once she jerked her chain and took me for a dive. It wasn't a good plan, though, because I have further memories of being dragged. The problem was that I was a Martens, with stubbornness running through my veins. I was every bit as stubborn as that little rebel, Sweetie. I simply refused to let her win, and I have the rope burn scars to prove it.

Sweetie eventually came around (as the weary angels gave a sigh of relief), and little miss sassy pants was ready for the show ring. Every girl needs a partner in crime; in 7th grade, she became mine. My cowboy boots kicked up sawdust as my hot pink wranglers waltzed into the show ring. I'd been to Jerry McPeak's "Be a Champ Show Cattle Camp" at Connors State College and was more confident in my game. Sweetie was by my side and we dominated every fair and every single show in between. It was a shutout. She won every single class. The judges would slap her Grand Champion time and time again, my face smeared in a perpetual smile.

Other than our stubbornness, Sweetie and I discovered we had something else in common: we both liked to win. Scratch that. We both loved to win. The trophies started invading every corner of my yellow bedroom on Bridgewater Lane. My newly decorated room made Sweetie's arrogance a little more tolerable to bear.

My first Grand Champion at the Arkansas State Fair, she made me a member of the Purple Circle Club. She taught me that hard work pays off if you are persistent. She also taught me that halter breaking can be hell on earth.

But, like all heifers, glory days must end and motherhood must begin. However, childbirth was not as easy for her as showing. Her first heifer was born crippled in her hindquarters, unable to prance around like her mother. She was colored up like her grandmother, Zula, amber with smoking eyes. We named her Sweet Dollars. She was a knockout. But she couldn't walk. My younger sister, Kiley, sat on the ground right beside her and cradled her, desperately trying to hug away her brokenness. She offered her heart because there was nothing else to offer. I learned that day not all brokenness is healed. We buried Sweet Dollars deep in the earth, and a touch of my own innocence went right into the grave alongside her. We thanked the Father for the place where there are no broken backs or broken hearts.

Sweetie had other babies. One day, Mom and I drove to Homer's to check on Sweetie to see if she'd had her latest calf. Homer Fry lived down the street and let Dad rent some additional land to run more cattle on. I had my bubble gum pink Hanimex 110 film camera ready to go. We found Sweetie easily enough, lying on the ground, the proud owner of a black bull calf. Mom took her some grain in a red bucket and started scratching her neck and telling her what a good momma she was.

The love language between fellow mothers was thick. I proceeded to take picture after picture. The neighborhood watch dog, who was really a 1400-pound cow aptly named Flo-Jo (after Olympic track and field winner Florence Griffith Joyner because of her speed) let out a bellowing war cry. She stormed out of the woods so fast she knocked us down to the ground before we even realized we were up and running. Because God alone numbers our days, Flo-Jo didn't trample us to death. My pink camera was also unscathed. Never let anyone tell you that cows aren't protective of one another. They love their herd and their own fiercely and with a passion that can either be admirable or terrifying, depending on which side of the fence you are on.

In the end, I realize I should have taught Sweetie Bible verses. Pride definitely goes before the fall. Fescue poisoning from a fungus in the grass got the best of her and she lost half of her tail in the process. Not only was her beauty marred, but she was unable to swat away the pesky horse flies. But it seemed her glory was now in motherhood and the freedom of an open field, instead of the show ring. And for that, I couldn't fault her one bit.

Kiley

"It's not the size of the dog in the fight,
it's the size of the fight in the dog."
Mark Twain

My sister, Kiley, was six years my junior and unlike me in every imaginable way. She could legitimately shoot a basketball while my single goal was for the opposing team. She was outgoing and loved attention. I, on the other hand, loved to be hidden away with a book in my hands. She thrived on adventure and trying new things while I road on people's coattails, making sure that not only had they paved the way, but that the way was safe.

Being a mere six years old and taking on a 1200-pound heifer was really no issue for Kiley. She led Coal Dream to the wash rack where we would daily bathe our show cattle in an attempt to grow their hair and teach it to lie correctly. The wash rack on Bridgewater Lane was simply a rod iron fence we tied them to. There was enough slope that the water would run off, keeping their hooves out of mud.

We grabbed our bottle of liquid sunshine labeled Joy and went to town. We sprayed the soap through the water hose to keep the suds from being too concentrated. Ideally, we would scrub one side, legs included, move to the other side, then do the head last, because who in their right mind—cows included--wants soap in their eyes?

Getting cows to move (at the speed and direction you desire) is the bane of every cattleman's existence, and the wash rack was no different. While being knit together in the womb, God gave Kiley a double portion of stubbornness. The fact that her gentle giant of a heifer wouldn't budge was really not a big deal to her. She marched herself into the shop and came out with the Hot Shot. This prodding device sends a zap into the animal, encouraging it to move along. The problem was that Kiley had yet to have a science class, and Coal Dream was soaking wet tied up to a dadgum lightning rod. The bellowing of that poor animal sent shockwaves straight up our spines. We couldn't wrestle that Hot Shot out of Kiley's hands fast enough. She, on the other hand, was all too proud of herself for getting Coal Dream to jump over the moon.

Despite all odds, Coal Dream lived to see another day. One time, we arrived at the Washington County Fair, and Kiley took off. We wondered why she would abandon us as we were trying to unload and set up. Minutes later, she returned with a whole slew of teenage cowboys ready to help us unload. The boys I couldn't even look in the eyes were eating out of the palm of her hand. Donned in light brown pigtails and bright Wranglers, she walked around like she owned the joint. Since she bought a horse from Uncle Jay at the age of five for a whopping $2, I had a sneaking suspicion she had a financial stake in the Washington County Fairgrounds, as well.

After we showed at the fair, on the last day, she gathered all of her friends, including Amanda, Andrea, and Craig Dewey. Being the leader of the pack, she led everyone onto the midway. They took over the whole place, riding rides and screaming like there was no tomorrow.

Wherever her boots landed, beams of light scattered.

She was a blaze to my soul as she taught me all manner of things regarding bravery and joy, boldness and laughter.

Bogie

"The most courageous act
is still to think for yourself. Aloud."
Coco Chanel

I was quickly learning that there were
various ways to make money in the cattle industry.
Some were the long game and others were the short
game. Show heifers could become cows which
would produce years of calves. Show bulls could be
turned to pasture with the herd or even have their
semen (housed in liquid nitrogen tanks) sold to the
highest bidder. Show steers were definitely the
short game. They lived for only a year and a half.
Their purpose was meat in the freezer: immediate
provision to feed a family.

The big boys played the steer game. There
was more money to be made if you did well enough
at the local and state fairs to end up in a Premium
Sale. Competitive as I was, and being twelve whole
years old, I decided it was time to put the big boys
in their place.

We named my first steer Humphrey Bogart.
I bought him; all Dad had to do was sign the check.
Bogie gave me my first and last drug hit of bidding
on cattle at auctions. It was an adrenaline rush
straight to my veins. Dad either took notice of the
increasing bid or my instant addiction and cut me
off from bidding after that.

After we got Bogie home, he started kicking
and I started shaking in my boots. Unlike horses,
cows kick without warning in just about any
direction, and my body was becoming the proof. In
order to keep him from kicking us while grooming
him for a show, we did something called tailing.
One person (I usually made Devin do it because it

took more strength than I could muster) would stand to the side of the chute and pick up the top portion of his tail and lift it straight up towards the sky. This would temporarily pinch a nerve and prevent him from kicking. This method helped me overcome my newfound fear of getting kicked into next week.

Columbia, Missouri, was a favorite winter show. Because it was held in either January or February, we were always guaranteed snow and lots of it. There were not enough insulated coveralls or wool socks to keep us warm, but we returned year after year. One year, the temperatures were so low that when we hit Bogie with the blow dryer, it instantly froze the droplets of water on his black coat, turning each hair into a piece of black diamond.

By the time autumn rolled around, Bogie had thawed back out and we were gearing up for our three fall shows which included the Washington County Fair in Fayetteville, the Arkansas Oklahoma State Fair in Fort Smith, and the Arkansas State Fair in Little Rock. Each fair progressed both in competition and higher paying premium livestock auctions. (Premium meant the exhibitor would keep the animal in order to proceed to future shows. The funds were a benefit to encourage the kids in showing future projects.) I viewed the auctions as a way of rewarding kids for their unseen hard work: breaking ice when the temperatures had dropped, mucking stalls, scooping out grain, washing and blowing them dry, flipping them onto a tilt table to trim their hooves, memorizing birthdates, cutting hair with the Andis and shearing clippers, giving vaccinations, running the foggers and fans in the dead of summer, swatting the guts out of each horse fly that dared land on their backs, and applying all sorts of creams and liquids and medicines to combat pink eye, ringworm, and warts. The world of showing cattle is very large, as vast as the number of horseflies we swatted away. The Arkansas Oklahoma State Fair had a certain rule that didn't sit well with my preteen mind. If I were to make auction (Grand Champion and Reserve Grand Champion were guaranteed this), then my steer would head straight to slaughter, hindering any more fairs. Now that Bogie was finally my pal, I had big dreams for us which included the Arkansas State Fair.

Deep down, I figured I had nothing to worry about. Who makes it to the Grand Champion drive with their very first steer? Imagine my surprise when I headed back into the ring for the choosing of the Grand and Reserve Grand Champions. Dad had forewarned me of the rule and told me that he would leave the decision to me. If I didn't get chosen as Grand, Dad told me I would have the freedom to leave the ring, and we would still be able to head to the State Fair later in October.

My stomach was in knots. I wasn't one to make a scene, but I knew I couldn't let Bogie get chosen that day. My little mind couldn't conceive of the fact that it might just be the end for him. Our plans included the State Fair, and we were so close! Besides, I was nowhere near ready to tell him goodbye.

The judge slapped another steer as Grand Champion and I hightailed it out of that sawdust covered ring so fast you would have thought he said "fire!" "Are you sure about this?" Dad asked me.

"Yes sir!" I replied. The judge thought I was confused and didn't understand that he still had to name another steer as Reserve Grand Champion. Dad defended my decision against every angry man that came into my path to argue my decision. Apparently, the judge was going to name Bogie Reserve Grand Champion, and he was not at all pleased with me for messing up his plans.

Dad stood by me. He gave me the freedom to make the decision, and he never doubted the decision after it was made. All along, he had been teaching me to make a decision and make it work.

The Arkansas State Fair came and went, and Bogie didn't do as well as I had hoped. He had peaked early. His time to shine was during the Arkansas Oklahoma State Fair, but I couldn't wrap my head around that as a twelve-year-old.

Dad never questioned my decision. He was smart like that. He transitioned me from blind obedience into taking responsibility in decision making. That day, Dad taught me to make a decision and stand by it, no matter the outcome. He instilled courage into me the day he let me decide whether Bogie lived or died. Looking back, I wish I had put myself under the authority of the judge, but I am thankful Dad gave me the chance to learn from my decisions.

A couple of months after the State Fair, we were all eating steak together at the bar. Dad had planned to tell me that it was a random cow they had butchered in case I brought it up.

Out of the clear blue sky, I asked, "Is this Bogie, Dad?"

"What if it is?" asked Dad, knowing he couldn't straight up lie.

"Well, I'd rather our family eat him than someone we don't know," I said.

And that was that. I passed the "eat your pet" contest with an A plus. Bring me all the steak, roast, hamburgers, ribs, brisket, liver, and even tongue. I was a growing girl and I had heard iron

27

and protein were beneficial things in a girl's diet.
We were blessed to have a freezer full of it.

Kirby

"Siblings are a volume of childhood memories;
a nostalgia that cannot be easily deleted."
Vincent Okay Nwachukwu

When I was seven, an exact replication of
my Dad popped out of my Mother's womb. As
Kirby made his entrance, he broke his collar bone,
due to his ten-pound frame. He looked like my
Dad, and later talked, walked, and stood like him,
as well. Our gentle giant would need an extra
measure of girth to be able to put up with Kiley
bossing him around, since being fifteen months
older immediately gave her the title of 'mommy.'

As a toddler, Kirby stole every heart in
Arkansas, with his blond curls and dimples the size
of asteroid craters. After putting on his Superman
pajamas, his red cape flying trailing behind, he
yelled, "Booter Boy to the rescue," saving us all
from imminent doom. He was such an endearing,
easy going child who entertained himself with
Teenage Mutant Ninja turtles and a yellow volt
battery powered four-wheeler.

My poor brother was surrounded on all
sides by sisters, but he learned to stand his ground;
the Martens' stubborn blood ran through his veins,
as well.

When he was five, Kirby pulled down his
little man Wranglers and had himself a nice little
pee. In the barn. At the fair. That little white moon
shined for all to see.

When Kirby was eight, Dad turned the baby
bull, Coal Power, over to him for a show, thinking
he could handle a bull that was mere months old.
At the Washington County Fair that year, the show
ring was split in two, so that beef and dairy could be

shown at the same time. Coal Power had a nurse momma that looked similar to a Holstein in the ring. This little bitty bull started foaming at the mouth and bolted for some lunch, leaving Kirby with a sawdust sandwich.

Cows are as good as dogs when it comes to judging the character and intentions of humans. Every cow that came in contact with Kirby knew he was as good as gold. Even Flo-Jo licked him through the fence. His steer, Red Rover, became a licker, as well. Red Rover was a classic case in the scientific experiment, "Pavlov's dog." Every time Kirby made a kissing noise, Red Rover licked him from his jaw line to his hair line: a cowlick in the very finest. The steer's famous tongue even made the paper one year.

One year at the State Fair, Kirby was trying to get his steer, Red Rover, from the nightly tie out area back to the barn. Red Rover broke away and dragged him. Kirby refused to let go, but his belt buckle he had just won for showmanship paid the cost. Every single bit of engraving was rubbed off, like a penny to a lottery ticket. His windbreaker jacket was so shredded Dad peeled it off of him, layer by layer like an onion, and put it straight into the trash. Red Rover did not get away that day, which made the annihilation of Kirby's wardrobe a little easier to bear.

Perhaps the best gift Kirby received from cow showing was his friend Craig Dewey. They shared dimples, shenanigans, and a good chase through the cow barn. Heart thieves, they were. Thirty plus years of friendship tells me that boys who show together stay together.

Showmanship

"These boots are made for walking, and that's just
what they'll do. One of these days these boots are
gonna walk all over you."
Lee Hazlewood

I quickly became the number one fan of
whoever invented the showmanship contest. I
loved working alone on things. School projects that
involved large groups of people made me cringe
because I never wanted someone else to be the
reason I failed or succeeded. Showing cattle fed my
individual drive, especially the showmanship
contest.

In truth, you won the contest while at home.
Showmanship was all about presenting your animal
in the best possible way to show off its best
qualities. It takes a lot of practice to get your
animal to be at ease and respond naturally to your
movements as well as the show stick. If you worked
at it enough, the animal would practically set itself
up when you entered the ring.

Oh, I was going to win. And win, I did. It
was the one place where politics, money, and
opinions were usually thrown out the door. I had
utter confidence because I knew if I followed the
rules, I could walk away with the trophy. Label me
a Pharisee, but I loved a good rule or two.

But, one day, I didn't win. We were at a
spring show, and Mr. Jary Douglas was the judge.
This was terrifying for many reasons, the top two
being his intimidation and the fact that I had a huge
crush on his son, Levi.

I quizzed myself on everything I thought he
might ask, hoping to be ready for whatever came
out of his mouth.

31

I led my black Limi heifer, Sweet Dreams, into the ring with all the confidence I could muster. That man made me nervous, despite all of my past showmanship awards. My show stick was in my left hand and my scotch comb was in my back right pocket. I entered the ring clockwise with a steady walk, following about 6 feet behind the steer in front of me. I walked to the left of Sweet Dreams so the judge would have a full-frontal view of her as she passed by him. I kept her halter shank tight, her head lifted at just the right height. My eyes bored into Judge Douglas until we arrived at the set-up spot. I made sure she wasn't standing in a hole. Then, I switched her halter to my left hand and started the magic. I pushed her head high, and then with the showstick, nudged the tender skin above her hooves, placing her front and hind legs at the correct distance.

I put my heifer's back leg that faced the judge farther back than the other one, which enhanced her natural muscling and volume. After Sweet Dreams moved her back leg too far, I used the show stick again, hooking the back of her foot until she placed it at the perfect spot. After this, I loined her topline with the show stick to smooth out the tiny hump and make her look as straight as possible. Then, Sweet Dreams stood in pacification as I gently scratched her belly with the show stick. Showmanship is all about showing off your animal's best traits, and I had her looking good.

Judge Douglas started inspecting each animal, touching the rib area and asking each youth a barrage of questions regarding them. I took a big breath when he got to me because I knew he was the captain of a tight ship.

"What's your heifer's birthdate?" asked the judge.

"3/18/89, sir," I said. Whew, that was an easy one, I thought.

"What's her weight?" he asked.

"1075 pounds, sir." I said.

"Who is her sire?" he implored.

"El Presidente, sir," I said. So far, so good.

"What percentage of protein are you feeding this heifer?" he asked. I didn't even know what he was asking me, much less the answer. I knew we fed her a mixture of grain, but goodness gracious, I didn't know math was required at dinnertime. Still, I was determined to have an answer for all of Judge Douglas's questions, so I flat out made something up. I think that's called lying.

"Six, sir," I croaked out.

"Six?" he almost laughed.

"Ummm, yes sir. Six," I said. Without a word, he left me with my lie and went on to the next showman.

I didn't win that day, but the loss taught me a greater truth: lying didn't look good on me. I humbly left it in Judge Douglas's ring forever, determined to just tell the truth from then on out.

And, yes, six percent protein is a tad bit low.

Mom

"Gilbert put his arm around them.
'Oh, you mothers!' he said. 'You mothers!'
God knew what He was about when He made you."
L. M. Montgomery

My Mom was the unsung hero of my childhood. There were three places she could usually be found: the kitchen, the laundry room, and on top of her made bed with her Bible and commentaries sprawled about.

The kitchen was the most important room of the house. Mom hovered, morning, noon, and night over our golden countertops, about to create something worth creating, like the Spirit of God hovered over the waters in the book of Genesis.

She fed us every single night with real food to nourish our growing bodies. Our taste buds led us to the curved bar where she loaded our earthen-colored Tupperware plates full of roast, mashed potatoes, brown gravy, carrots, green beans, yeast rolls, chocolate cake, and cups filled to the brim with sweet iced tea. We praised God for the bounty, and licked our plates clean. We weren't rich, but we always ate like kings and queens.

After eating, we dumped our wicker barstools over and pounded them like a game of Whack-A-Mole, until all the crumbs had fallen to the ground. We rolled the carpet sweeper back and forth over the brown carpet, then I took over the bar with basic arithmetic and American President research papers, willing my eyes to stay open despite the food coma Mom had induced. Baby Schuyler Amelia sat on the bar in her carrier, babbling me back to reality.

If she wasn't in the kitchen, Mom was probably two steps away, knee deep in a mountain of manure-stained wranglers and coveralls, washing load after load, feeding the monster that could never be satiated. She wasn't just washing the clothes of a family of seven; she was washing the clothes of children who wore school and chore outfits, plus those of a baby who had blow outs and spit ups. If she had earned a dollar for every single load she ever did, her billions would put Oprah to shame. Not to worry, though, I know there is treasure stored up for her in heaven.

She didn't just keep us clean or nourish our bodies; she fed our souls.

If she wasn't in the kitchen or the laundry room, then I could often find her on her bed. Her Bible, along with every commentary ever written, was at home beside her. She filled notebook after notebook with prayers and with everything God was teaching her. Her room was her own private seminary with God as her primary teacher. During this time, God literally gave her songs, complete with melodies and lyrics to share with our church body. Seeing her with the invisible Almighty always gave me peace. She came out of those moments refueled and ready to offer us the grace that we so desperately needed.

Mom found her strength to raise five children by going to God not just on a daily basis, but breath by breath. Those two were tight. Her prayers over her children kept them from being trampled by cattle and all the other dangers involved in living on a small farm. Her intercession brought the free gift of salvation to each of her children. Her warring spirit allowed each of those children to serve God and use their giftings for His glory alone. She never backed down on truth even when the culture started saying things that were contradictory to the Word of God. She loved each of us well enough to discipline us and not leave us in rebellion; I have a broken blue hairbrush to prove it.

She was my shoulder to cry on when whatever cute cowboy flavor of the day wouldn't notice me. She brush hogged at Homer's when Dad was unable to get the job done. She was the fashionista behind all of my cute showing outfits, including the black studded tux shirt that sparkled under the sale night lights. She managed to get a family of seven packed for each show, knowing we might need extra clothes for premium sales, Purple Circle Banquets, or the occasional face plant into a pile of manure.

Who knows what all she sacrificed along the way so Dad could buy grain, tool boxes, entry fees, grooming supplies, hair dryers, halters, trailers, and chutes. I doubt that showing cattle was her personal dream, but she gave up a life to make it happen for us.

One time when Dad was unable to get off work, Mom loaded the Suburban and trailer like it was a Tetris game, got behind the wheel, and hauled all manner of children and bovine to a show in Conway. I could see her gasping for air on the narrow toothpick lanes. She pulled into the fairgrounds, parked in the middle of the road, let out a "Praise the Lord!" and sent us after someone who could actually park the giant rig.

But even my superhero of a mother had her limits.

For a solid year, Dad drove from our home in Fayetteville, AR, all the way down to Shreveport, LA, every week. He had gone to work for United Built Homes to manage their lumberyard. I was in the 8th grade. Dad would come home on Fridays and go back on Sundays. Six hours one way. Every single week.

While I am sure Dad was lonely, my Mom was left with the hard work: five children and a herd of cattle. Devin and I fed, watered, and bathed our show cattle every day. Dad had bought a black Limousin bull, C.D., which stood for Cash Deposits. The goal was to make money off of his offspring. But fatherhood never became part of his story, and his name became an ironic, even cruel joke.

Devin and I were doing our best to lead C.D. from one area to the tie up spot in the back of the barn. That bull was too obstinate. We tried all of our tricks, but he simply wouldn't budge. I went to get Mom, but she couldn't get him to move, either. It was no use. We decided to go eat supper and try again later. C.D. was a bear to catch, so we didn't dare set him loose. There was a free-standing pole that we tied him to, knowing full well it wasn't the safest option, but thinking it was our only option.

When the three of us returned from supper, we had a dead bull on our hands. C.D. had circled the pole over and over again until his halter was so tight that it choked the life out of him. While we dined, he suffocated himself.

"Shit! Shit! Shit!" screamed my Mom as she kicked the black bull, willing him back to life. Her words sucked the breath right out of me because I had never heard her cuss before, and it made me realize what a dire situation this really was. Dad wasn't around to help us know what to do, or better yet, to do it. What on earth were we going to do with a one-ton dead bull?

Later that evening, Uncle Jay and Uncle Karl came to our rescue. They strung up C.D. in the shop, drained his blood, and sent him to the slaughterhouse.

Mom, Devin, and I felt helpless. The weight of the loss was on each one of us. We were responsible but also fully aware that the burden of keeping large obstinate bulls alive was beyond our capabilities.

We soon moved to be with Dad in Shreveport.

Ninth Grade

"Make no mistake, adolescence is a war.
No one gets out unscathed."
Harlan Coben

Ninth grade shocked the system. All that was known: Bridgewater, junior high, church, two sets of grandparents, friends, and twelve years of childhood got smaller and smaller in the rearview mirror as we packed our grey Suburban, moving truck, and cattle semi-trailer and headed south to a state that was so different, it had parishes instead of counties.

A tiny dot on the northwest corner of Louisiana encased my memories of the next year. Haughton, population 1700, a small suburb of Shreveport, became our dwelling from 1991-1992. Mom and Dad chose small town America as opposed to the hustle and bustle of the big city. Our cattle needed land and our hearts would need wide open spaces as well: a place of haven amidst the terror of new.

We lived on Elm Street, and to this day, I have an occasional nightmare about our brief jaunt in that town. The irony isn't lost on me.

I was never a dancer (my Dad called me Lulu, for crying out loud) but my Mom was doing her best to guard my heart as we made this huge transition. She requested a try out on the high step dance line for me so I might possibly make some friends before school started. Flexibility was never an issue, but keeping time to choreography was another thing. I finagled my way through the special try out and *somehow* made the Haughton Highsteppers. Mom simply wanted me to belong as we moved to a new place. God laughed that day.

I only danced on the high school football field one time. Every week, we had to make the cut in order to dance. I never made it. The one time I danced was during a special American Patriotic presentation where every highstepper lined up. I was so nervous I fell over during one of the moves where I had to be on my knees.

The first day of high school was something else. The upper classmen highsteppers roasted and initiated the freshmen by dressing them up however they desired. My group turned me into a 70's brown polyester outfitted, mile-high beehive adorned, smoky black eye lined hippy. I knew no one other than the dance team, and the first day was torture as everyone stared at me and whispered, "*Who is thaaaat?*" I was on display for all to see and I begged God for a sinkhole to open up and swallow me, beehive and all. He said no.

One moment of rejection stands out above the others. My brother, Devin, was a senior at the same school; and some twins on the dance team had their eyes set on him, as he was tall, dark, handsome, *and* new in small-town-America. They invited him to a pool party hosted by their church youth group and for whatever reason, I was the default tag along. They were the only girls there I knew, so it seemed reasonable that I would attach myself at their identical hips. They had other plans. Every time I would swim over to either Raven-haired #1 or Raven-haired #2, they would immediately (and rather quickly) swim away. I was left all alone in a crowded pool of hormone-infested chlorine water. Once again, God said no and didn't allow the ground to eat me up. Having nowhere to hide is the strictest form of punishment for an introvert living in fear.

God never once opened up that ground, but He did allow my hamstring to get pulled later that year. My dance team foe, Heather, who pretty much hated me for a reason unbeknownst to me, was helping me stretch while standing against a wall. She thought I said "more" when I really said "stop" --because, clearly, they sound the same--and abruptly pushed my leg into my nose. My hamstring let out a series of cuss words worse than any my innocent ears had ever heard. After the pulled muscle, I needed recovery and rest. I quit the Haughton Highsteppers.

Bile rises when I think of that first kiss. His last name was Newton, but his friends called him Fig. Prom was coming up, and he, a junior, asked me, a freshman. A shiny dress, limo, and fancy dinner waited, so I said yes. I hardly knew him, but we were going as a large group, so I figured I was safe. All was well until he followed me into my dark house and stuck his tongue down my tonsils. That was the last of Fig.

It is funny how kids will excel at whatever gift God gives them. I was chosen, as a freshman, to sing "O' Holy Night" at the Rose Garden Christmas light display in Shreveport. I could not dance, but I could belt out my favorite Christmas song to the hundreds there enjoying the light display. I will never forget the brisk air, the myriad of twinkling lights, my family all together, and the promise of future buds on each rose bush.

About halfway through the year, I got sent to the Principal's office. I loved a good rule handbook, but Haughton High had one rule that was beyond absurd in its context. The girls could not wear shorts of any length, but they could wear tube tight miniskirts that barely covered their buttocks. I cannot handle stupidity or injustice, so, one day, I wore dark green plaid dress shorts that went all the way to my knees, as well as black opaque tights underneath. I looked more nun than hooker, but to the principal I was sent, nonetheless. I did not have the guts to explain the ridiculous reasoning of their pharisaical law, so I cried instead. I got off with a warning and left my shorts in my pink closet on Elm Street.

Chief Blackmon was my favorite instructor. He was about five feet tall, with sprouts of white follicular tufts, begging for their daily shave. He donned large black spectacles that reminded me of the JFK days. Chief Blackmon taught us about cumulus clouds, drill lines, and respect. He told us to assume nothing because when one assumes, it creates an "ass" out of "u" and "me." That is one line that has forever stayed with me; I'm pretty sure the cussing made it stick.

Chief Blackmon won my heart by making me drill sergeant of our class. He was someone who decided to believe in the new girl instead of shame or ignore her. He forced me out of my comfort zone, but also launched me into an area of unexpected success. To this day, I can still hear his booming voice: "Leeeft, leeeft, left, right, leeeft."

Every Thursday, rain or shine, we cadets donned our navy-blue uniforms, complete with name tags, wings, cords, and hard-earned ribbons. My ribbons are packed in the attic, sandwiched between my retainers and hand written letters from my Arkansas childhood friends, who were shockingly able to live their lives without me.

My brother, Devin, ended up joining the Air Force after graduating, thanks to the Haughton JROTC program.

When Miss Piggy showed up in our backyard unannounced, I aimed to keep her. A police officer came to our door inquiring about her, but I honestly don't remember what I told him. Mom and Dad were out of town trying to save my heifer Sky and the policeman practically scared the metal braces right off my teeth. So, if he asked if we had a stray pig (unlike cows, pigs weren't allowed in the city limits no matter how much land one owned,) I may have told the truth or I may have lied straight up. I honestly don't remember. All I know is I got to love that pig until she ended up in our freezer, and then I may have loved her even more, because...BACON. God's provision often reveals itself in odd ways, and she was just what our family of seven was hungry for.

When it came to livestock, raising cows was my specialty, so naturally, I haltered Miss Piggy with a cow rope halter and proceeded to break her so that I could lead her around like I did with my show cows. She never quite surrendered, but she did take to acting like a cow in other ways, like climbing into the calf grain feeder, front legs propped up on the metal railing, munching away. She was the best (and only) pig I ever had.

There seemed to be more of God on our plot of land than in the tiny First Baptist Church we attended. Not that there was anything wrong with that church, but the glory of God in that sanctuary was nothing compared to sitting on the banks of our pond, reeling in catfish after catfish as a family. Before this, I did not know that fishing could be so sacred. To see Kiley's face light up after she hooked a big one. To laugh at Kirby, begging to throw fat fistfuls of dog food, beckoning fish to the surface. To behold Schuyler Amelia in sunkissed pigtails, my motherly-self willing her two-year-old self away from the murky depths. Every detail was pure glory.

To have one single thing that brought all of us together—that even allured Pops, Granny, Nana, and Grandad from six hours away—to share in something as simple as casting rods and feasting on the bounty; it was sacred, indeed. In a time of change, uncertainty, and even cruelty, our pond was our sanctuary and a haven away from it all. God used whiskered bottom-dwellers to give us hope that all would be fine. We worshiped well on those banks as we exhaled the world and inhaled shalom.

Sky

"Look after your sheep
and cattle as carefully as you can."
Proverbs 27:23

Home was supposed to be my haven, but even the small farm was bringing sorrow. I am the one that killed her. Lana, that is. She was our most expensive cow (thousands and thousands of dollars) and I inadvertently sent her six feet under, her grave dug by backhoe and hot tears. Our barn in Haughton had two large sliding doors, one in the front that faced the back of the house, and another that overlooked our land. The doors allowed us to store all kinds of things inside: tractors, cattle trailers, and show cattle equipment. It also housed uncovered barrels of grain, meant to be dished out about half a bucket at a time. After I did chores one evening, I shut the front sliding door but accidentally left the back one open. Lana got into the barn and literally feasted herself to death on the grain while I slept the night away.

The weight of an 1800 pound black Limousin cow sat squarely on my 118 pound teen self. It was a burden almost too great, this murder of mine. How on earth would I ever dig myself out from the suffocating blow of one mere act of forgetfulness? I would have done anything to take it back. My only consolation was my parents' gracious response which eventually taught me I could let it go, as well.

It's a toss-up on whether killing Lana or kissing Fig was the final exhale of my childhood. Both sucked the oxygen right out, only leaving behind the taste of adulthood that I wasn't sure I was prepared for. One day I was a child and the next, I simply wasn't.

Lana wasn't the only cow that indulged in grain that night. My show heifer, Red Sky in the Morning, did as well. Her stomach started shutting down as a result. She was dying. Mom and Dad loaded her up and drove through the night to arrive at LSU at 6 a.m. the next morning. I was left in charge of the kids, which must have been a major act of insanity on my parents' part, since I had just killed their best cow.

While I tended the farm and kept the policeman from taking my stray pig away, the vets at LSU proceeded to cut open my heifer and rinse her stomach out with a water hose. There was a cow on the premises that had a fistula—a window into her stomach. The vets removed fifteen gallons of stomach acids from that cow and pumped it into Sky's stomach. Then they sewed her back up. After the surgery, my parents left her in the care of the vets so she could recover.

Two weeks later, I drove with Dad back to LSU and we brought her home. I shudder to think what the vet bills were, but to me, all that mattered was that my baby had been saved.

Miracle of miracles, Sky didn't just live, but she went on to be grand Limousin heifer at the Louisiana State Fair. I was ultra-protective of Sky after her surgery. Later that fall, I was back on my home state fairgrounds, ready to show her off, five-inch scar running down her side, and all. I tied her to a post near the show ring and stepped away to help Kiley and her heifer get set up. When I turned back around, Sky was gone!

I looked everywhere and finally spotted Sky being shown in the ring by some unfamiliar man. He was walking towards me with a blue ribbon in his hand, having just won with Sky in a much younger class. "Give me back my heifer!" I screamed.

"This isn't your heifer," he argued.

"See this scar," I shouted. "Does the heifer you have been hired to show have a scar running down her middle?"

"No," he said sheepishly. He placed Sky's rope in my hands and stormed away.

Nobody steals Sky Baby for his own glory.

We went on to get second in the class she was supposed to participate in. It was a win for me, though, because she had already taken Grand Champion at county, and above all else, was alive.

Dad later sold Sky and her baby at a cow sale in Durant, Oklahoma. I hoped the three grand he got for them put a small dent into paying off those vet bills. Selling Sky was like taking a cyanide pill, but her continued life managed to trump the death I felt after I told her goodbye.

Precious Moments

"I will not cause pain without allowing
something new to be born, says the LORD."
Isaiah 66:9

When Doll Zula dropped her newest baby
heifer on April 18, 1992, the topsy turvy world of 9th
grade righted itself again. She was colored just like
her mama: auburn hair, black nose, and dark eyes
rimmed in heavy black liner. It was love at first
sight. Precious Moments was her name and she
definitely lived up to it, bringing me purple ribbon
after purple ribbon in the show ring and solace in
the barn. For the next couple of years, she was a
constant in my swirl of teenage girl emotions.

I liked her, loved her really, for a myriad of
reasons. Precious was all things good, but she had
an air of confidence about her that I found
appealing and even coveted. If she were human,
and sometimes I wondered if maybe she was, she
would be someone you would never want to mess
with. Get on her bad side, and she might thumb (or
hoof) that beautiful black nose at you forever.

At Nationals that summer in Fort Worth,
Texas, Zula and Precious won Reserve Grand
Champion Cow-Calf Pair. It was the first time Zula
had ever been shown. Who knew you could halter
break a seven-year-old cow then watch her get
second in the nation at her very first show? Chris
Sweat led Zula and I led Precious, side by side. That
pair stole the National Junior Limousin title like it
was nothing. It was truly a Cinderella story for us
all.

Nationals that summer may have been my
favorite cow show. The experience was larger than
life and yet, I seemed to fit right in. Mom and Dad

bought me a hot pink and teal windbreaker jacket with my Reserve Champion status embroidered on the back. I was as proud of that jacket as if I'd given birth to it. The week of festivities concluded with a champion awards dinner. I received a leather engraved briefcase, a leather notepad holder, and a purple banner the size of the host state. After dinner, we ended the night with a dance. Christ Sweat took me in a hallway to teach me how to country line swing dance. We came back out, two stepping this way and that, until everyone cleared the floor and let us swing. Just clean, fun dancing. I was so elated I counted 5024 Limi heifers in order to fall asleep that night.

All of the livestock stalls at Nationals were decorated in yellow ribbons, supporting our troops over in Desert Storm. A sense of hope consumed me as I walked the aisles looking at all the cattle and ribbons. I felt unified with a greater cause and I was also filled with the anticipation of moving back home to Northwest Arkansas. I was one happy heifer.

As Precious grew older, people would make fun of her, calling her a Guernsey (which is a type of dairy cow) instead of a Limi, the beef kind that she really was. I wanted to fight back (Nobody puts Baby in the corner!!!), then I would remember that sassy pants Precious did not need anyone to come to her defense. She knew she was good, and she turned a deaf ear to all the stupid talk (Superhuman, I tell you). As college started and I quickly aged out of the legal show age, I would let the tears fall. Perhaps it was Precious I missed the most, the two of us against the world, knocking down anything that attempted to get in our way.

Springdale

"There's always a bit of suspense about the particular way in which a given school year will get off to a bad start."

Frank Portman

The summer we moved back to Northwest Arkansas was the very balm of Gilead. We rented a house from the Reddish family while we looked for one to buy. The house had a pool! It was the one and only summer we ever had a pool, and we were in chlorine heaven. Devin had left for Air Force Basic, but Kiley, Kirby, Amelia, and I would splash and play the days away. The creepy crawly pool cleaner fascinated us so much we spent hours watching it magically suck away debris. After a rough patch in Louisiana, it was good to just be a kid and play again.

But what was constantly on my mind was that we had moved to Springdale instead of Fayetteville. All of my friends were in Fayetteville. I had only met one Springdale person my age through 4-H: Natalie Allen, whose mom, Helen, was the director. School was fast approaching, and I had zero friends to help me enter the world called high school. Even though I was happy to be back in Arkansas, I was secretly terrified.

On the first day of school, I put one foot in front of the other, eventually finding myself in Mrs. Flynt's English class. She ended up being a God-send of a teacher who taught me all manner of things, and she used good ol' Flannery O' Conner to do it. While I was trying to figure out how I was a Springdale Bulldog instead of a Fayetteville Bulldog, I sat and soaked her in.

Sadly, English class ended and I later had to venture out into the lunchroom. I saw the long hot lunch line and reality hit like an arrow into the bull's eye. "I have absolutely no one to eat lunch with. There is no way on God's green earth I am going to go sit down by myself and eat lunch," I thought to myself.

I sidestepped out of that lunch line like it was the green mile and found the women's bathroom as fast as my legs would go. I had never skipped a meal in fifteen years of life, but fear trumped food that day. I locked myself in the stall and sat down on the stool, incessantly staring at my watch. I was willing to starve myself, but I wasn't willing to be late for my next class. Good girls just aren't tardy.

Evidently, the rumblings of my stomach weren't too noticeable that afternoon because no teacher turned me into child protective services for the blatant hunger I thought for sure was plastered all over my face. After school, I charged into the house with one singular mission: food. I breezed past my parents' quizzical looks and yanked open the refrigerator door. I grabbed the first piece of Tupperware I could find: giant meatballs. Mom's meatballs weren't the typical Spaghetti-O's sized meatballs. They were the size of a fist and to die for. I wasn't used to missing meals, so I did what any normal starving person would do. I shoved a cold one in each cheek, chipmunk style, and started chewing. Fast.

All the while, my parents stared and tentatively asked how my first day of high school was. I blubbered forth a hot mess of tears, anger, frustration, insecurity, and humiliation. Snot ran down my face and I couldn't even talk because I kept choking on the three pounds of hamburger meat I had recklessly shoved into my face.

"Becke', maybe we've messed up by switching you to Springdale," Dad said.

"I'll be fine, Dad. I just need one blasted person to eat lunch with. One single friend. That's all I need," I choked out.

God must have immediately intervened because I never hid in the bathroom or missed another meal again. God, in fact, brought me countless friends at Springdale High. I filled my diary with the names of Charity, Amy, Candi, Heather, Jennifer, Jene', Jesse, Rebecca, Cara, and Cherish, time and time again.

I quickly became a headbanger due to exhausting trigonometry and algebraic equations. I sat on my bed, day after day, homework in hand, banging my head against the wall in frustration. I didn't care what my teacher, Mrs. Burlingame said, letters didn't belong in math. Period. I needed a place to run away to, and Red Oak Estates became my haven. Nestled in forty acres on top of a hill in Tontitown sat the prettiest view. Countless red oaks splattered the landscape. Dad built a barn and for the next few years, our show cattle had a new place to call home.

The barn was about fifteen minutes from the house we bought on Evelyn Street in Springdale. After school, Kiley and Kirby piled into my car and we headed to God's country. On the drive, I exhaled algebraic equations and inhaled the freedom of winding roads that swayed to the rhythm of Trisha, Garth, and Shania.

Fall was the smell of Red Oak Estates. Countless leaves waltzed before my Mercury Topaz, beckoning me to the barn, like the song of a siren. I got out of my car, opened the tack room, and

52

breathed in the smell of grain, the scent grounding me to reality as the earthy sweetness invaded my senses, taking over the stale putridness of the classrooms. Mice were never a problem, thanks to Mama Z, our Russian Blue cat.

Kiley, Kirby, and I caught Ajax, Mr. Clean, Comet, Precious, Haisey, and Touch of Coal, and tied them up at the wash rack. The lineup was a bona fide car wash: we went through hundreds of gallons of water and suds a day, each animal coming out squeaky clean. While bathing them, we squashed horse flies that landed, guts flying like red fireworks. We apologized to our cows for hitting them, but I know they were thankful to have one less nuisance around. After baths, we combed them and blew them dry. Then, we led them back to their individual stalls. I dished out grain while Kiley and Kirby gave them fresh water.

One day, while driving home, we encountered a massive snake slithering along the country pavement. I purposefully ran over it and then put my Topaz in reverse and backed over it again. I repeated this process of annihilation about ten times until I was confident the snake was deader than Elvis. No snake was going to hurt my sister and brother. I must have been oblivious to the fact that snakes can't crawl through the metal of a vehicle weighing over a ton traveling at a decent speed. Nevertheless, no sibling was getting bit on my watch.

There are two things that make the life of a cattle rancher in winter a bit tricky: cows must always have fresh hay to eat and cows must always have unfrozen water to drink. Even though we lived fifteen minutes away, a snowstorm didn't cancel the need for cows to eat and drink.

In the middle of February 1993, I woke up to a cascade of snow. "School's out! School's out!" Kiley, Kirby, and Amelia sang.

"Come on, Lulu, let's go run some errands and go feed cows," Dad said. I was already bored, so I hopped into the grey Suburban with him. We drove to Ozark Electric and then downtown to Layman's Hardware store. Layman's knew how to treat their customers well, and I gladly took some complimentary hot chocolate and popcorn. After my mid-day snack, we headed to Tontitown, where our cows waited for hay, grain, and water.

We turned onto Highway 112 and came down a hill and then started sliding out of control when we hit the bridge. The Suburban flipped over onto my side and scraped over the concrete edge meant to keep one from landing in the creek.

"Becke', are you alright?" Dad was hovering in the air above me, his buckle keeping him from falling onto me.

"I think so, Dad," I said. All I could smell was gasoline. The generator was in the back of the suburban and gas was leaking out everywhere. Maybe I had watched too many movies, but I was terrified we were going to blow up. After we somehow crawled out of Dad's window, we stood on the icy embankment. Thanks to mobile phones and Contel Cellular, Dad called his friend, David Starkey, to see if he could come get us. Then, he called a wrecker and a policeman.

The cop terrified me more than the gas leak and the cold seeping into my bones. It was as if he had no heart. Dad sat in his car for a hot minute and then David took us home. I am sure our cows got fed and watered that day, because even major accidents don't prevent them from needing to eat and drink.

I remember being able to remain calm because Dad was calm. His peace covered me like a warm blanket straight out of the dryer. The Suburban, however, was a goner.

My friend, Anita, lost her dad in another car accident the very same day. The fact that he died and we lived was almost too much for my teen mind to process. Although I will never quite grasp the sovereignty of God, it was a good starting point in trying to learn.

Quiz Bowl

"There's something you must always remember.
You are braver than you believe, stronger than you
seem, and smarter than you think."
Winnie the Pooh

All high school members of the Arkansas
Junior Cattleman's Association were highly
encouraged (i.e.: made) to form a team and enter
the State Cattleman Quiz Bowl in Fort Smith. I had
no time for such nonsense, as I was trying to
memorize all 68 lines of Hamlet's soliloquy by
Shakespeare. "To be, or not to be, that is the
question" was just the first line. I was also trying to
ace AP Physics, which was no easy feat since math
had not just taken over the beautiful world of
letters, but invaded science as well. Maintaining
my 4.4 GPA was my hopes of getting a college
scholarship. The quiz bowl was not offering me a
scholarship. Priorities.

But we were "encouraged" to sign up, so I
did. There ended up being enough kids in
Washington County to form two teams. Esteemed
Team A consisted of Caleb, Bonnie, and David, the
kids that were actually studying and had the best
chance of taking state. Lowlife Team B consisted of
Jennifer, Danita, and myself, the lower rungs of the
educational ladder.

The night before the quiz bowl, panic set in.
I absolutely hated losing and couldn't bear the
thought of showing up with a dunce hat on my
head. Buried beneath Hamlet and Physics, I found
the pamphlets and study material the 4-H leaders
had provided and started cramming it into my head
as fast as it would go, prying my sleepy eyes open

with pliers. "Short term memory, don't fail me now!" I prayed as I finally let myself go to sleep.

When we arrived at the convention center, I had butterflies in my stomach dancing to the tune of Reba: "Here's your one chance, Fancy, don't let me down." I hated entering new situations where I didn't know what to expect. But, instead of finding a bathroom to hide in, I clung to my teammates and stuck my face back into the pamphlets.

They placed opposing teams in various rooms. Each room had two tables at the front, complete with personal buzzers. My nerves had an unlimited supply of ammo that day. I kept calling for a cease fire, but they just wouldn't let up. The feeling was worse than any Grand Champion drive I had ever been a part of.

The judge sat before us with questions. He had a look of amusement on his face that I wanted to wipe off with a grease towel. I think he was delighted at how terrified we were. After dishing out the rules, he began.

"Question 1: Name three breeds of beef cattle," inquired the judge. I heard a buzzer that sounded before I could even process the question. It was not from my table. "Hereford, Angus, and Charolais," said some opposing girl with the biggest smirk. "You are correct," replied the judge.

"Question 2: What does polled mean?" asked the judge. Shoot. I had forgotten my own name by this point. I asked Jesus to come and rapture me right then and there. Another buzzer blared from far away. "A cow born without horns," replied a guy from the other side. "You are correct" said the judge.

"OK, these are not even the hard questions. Enter the game now, crazy girl," I said to myself.

"Question 3: What are the three best grades of beef?" I slammed the buzzer, which surprisingly brought me a rush as high as bidding on cattle. Little did my opponents know what they were in for. "Prime, choice, and select," my ears heard my shaky voice say. I knew it was the right answer before the judge even approved it because I could talk steak. "You are correct," said the judge. One down, 5 million to go. I got this.

"Question 4: What is the gestation period of a cow?" Danita slammed her buzzer and shouted out, "285 days." "You are correct," said the judge. Here we were. Killing it with the pregnancy and steak-eating questions. Team Girl was made for this.

"Question 5: "What is a male animal that has been castrated before sexual maturity called?" Some boy on the other team slammed down his fist as if he were knocking away the castration knife away from his own balls. "Steeeeer!" was his warrior cry. "You are correct" said the judge. Well, what can I say? I can't relate to that kind of fear. He earned that one.

"Question 6: What are four types of high energy source feeds?" the judge asked. I slammed it. "Barley, oats, corn, and wheat." The judge once again said, "You are correct." Well, duh, we were talking about food again.

"Question 7: What feed helps your animal grow and build muscle?" Jennifer slammed her hand down and said, "protein!" "You are correct," said the judge. We three girls must have been hungry that morning.

"Question 8: What are three parasites that affect cattle?" asked the judge. Castration boy piped up, "ticks, lice, and horn flies." Of course, he was correct. This parasite was getting on my ever-loving nerves. Time to swat him away forever.

"Question 9: What are the four parts of a ruminant's stomach in order?" asked the judge. I was made for this. I loved words and spelling and pronunciation and all things order. "The rumen, the reticulum, the omasum, and the abomasum," I said with pride. "You are correct," said the judge.

Wam, bam, thank you mam! And that is how Lowlife Team B won the first round.

Our underrated Team B went through four more rounds of this exhilarating gauntlet, each round becoming increasingly difficult. We kept advancing and somehow evaded Team A all day long. And then, we were given the news that the two teams that were advancing to the championship round were none other than the esteemed Team A and lowly Team B, all from almighty Washington County.

There is a point in time when you have to decide for yourself whether you are going to believe what someone else says of you is true (you aren't good enough to be on the best team) or listen to your own dialogue (by golly, I've helped us make it to the championship round and deserve to sit at the table, no matter how I was previously labeled.)

The arsenal of ammo kept firing at my nerves as we climbed onto a platform as tall as the Tower of Babel, so all the teams and parents could see the contestants. I despised being on display, but I loved winning even more, so I sat myself down and tried not to crap my britches.

Team A brought their A game. In the second to last question, we were down 20 to 35. I answered the next question and the bonus after that which allowed us to end the game in a tie. The judge asked the tie-breaking final question in slow motion. I knew our only chance of winning was to slam on my buzzer and figure out the answer in the solid second that followed.

My buzzer went off first which left me as a deer in the headlights because in that split second, I wasn't sure if I knew the third part of the question. I listed off the first two answers, and then the voice of a muse took over. The answer came forth from the depths of who knows where, almost in spite of myself. To this day, I don't remember the final question or the answer, only that it was the most surreal victory of my life.

On the day of the State Championship Cattleman's Quiz Bowl, I learned that lowlifes can rise to the surface like cream if only given the chance. (And maybe by swatting away a few pesky parasites throughout the day.)

Jennifer, Danita, and I got red puffy quiz bowl champion coats, t-shirts, and five hundred dollars. The powers that be made us split the money with Team A, to celebrate the fact that we were one unified county, and all.

I was pretty sure that we had just smoked the pants off of Team A, but I kept my mouth shut when I divvied up our earnings.

I knew who the winners were.

I'm betting Team A did, as well.

12th Grade

"But all good things must come to an end—and I
hear the greatest things tend to end quicker than
they started."
Sarah Mello

In the fall of 1994, I entered my senior year.
The county fair always coincided with the first week
of school, which made for a shot vial full of insanity.
I started out taking Calculus, but got so behind
while at the fair that I dropped out of the class the
second week. I didn't even need the math credit,
and I was learning I didn't have to eat punishment
soup on a daily basis.

At the Washington County fair, my black
baldy steer, Shadrach, who looked like a giant fluffy
panda bear, got Grand Champion steer. He
brought a whopping $3100 at the premium auction.
Meshach, my other steer, got 3rd in his class. Laney
Lou and Precedence got Reserve Grand Champion
Limousin heifer and bull.

Cara Parnell, Rebecca Shipley, and I put on
matching white bedazzled tux shirts and bright
Wranglers and sang "Maybe it was Memphis" in the
Talent Contest of the fair. We won our division and
had the best girl time of our lives doing it.

After the fair, I settled back into school, sans
Calculus. My course load was insane, including
three AP classes. I studied incessantly for the ACT,
trying to get my score up high enough for a
scholarship. I even ditched country music for
Mozart, in hopes that it might make me smarter. I
finally got a 26, which landed me some scholarship
opportunities.

The fall was an F-5 tornado. After school, I
drove to the barn to wash two steers, a heifer, and a

61

bull. Then, I hightailed it to Sbarro to make pizzas at the rate of $5.50 an hour. After that, I headed home to cram Moby Dick, All Region vocal music, and AP Physics into my brain. On Wednesdays, I went to youth group. Weekends were for church, football games, work, and the social life that seniors must maintain.

Every October, the State Fair opened its arms in a wide-open embrace. It was as if this culminating fair knew how hard we had worked and rewarded our lungs with the first brisk breath of fall. Win or lose, we had arrived and we were going to soak up every minute.

The excitement traveled like electricity through our boots and hit the pavement as we unloaded the cattle we longed to show off. Kirby, Kiley, and I started making the cattle beds. We grabbed plenty of bags of fresh shavings and ripped them open with glee, spreading the contents in every direction and packing it down like cups of brown sugar. Due to the weight of cattle and the rustling around they would do, their beds would disintegrate faster than an Alka-Seltzer placed in water. We put plenty out and built the bed higher in the front so they wouldn't lay in their own manure before we had a chance to shovel it away.

After bringing our show cows to their newly made beds, we unloaded and set up the chutes, show box, and other equipment. We rewarded ourselves with a nap taken on the shavings, right next to our cows.

Shadrach had developed a calcium deposit on his shoulder, which gave him an ugly pop up knot, but we were confident we could cover it up with his panda hair. He placed second in his class, behind what ended up being the Grand Champion overall. I was sad I didn't make it to the Grand drive, but God wasn't done yet. Only 18 out of the 130 steers being shown that year made the premium sale. We barely made the cut, coming in at 17th. Most steers were bringing an average of $600. I was floored when we entered the auction ring and the bids kept increasing. Thanks to Mr. Myers, who bought on behalf of Tyson Foods, Shadrach brought $2000, which was the 6th highest in the sale. It was a beautiful miracle to me. It taught me that God's ways are so much higher than our own. We simply can't box God in. He is in the heavens and He does as He pleases.

Laney Lou got second in her class, also behind the heifer that ended up being Grand. Meshach got 8th.

That year, it was Precedence's time to shine. He was my 2000-pound black Limousin bull. Showing bulls was a powerful thing. If you could manage a bull that had a wide range of lady friends all around, then you could handle just about any animal. The use of a nose ring sure didn't hurt, either. In 1994, the year of our Lord, Precedence was king. He won not just the junior show title, but the open show one as well, setting the precedence as our only bull to do so. We went back to the Purple Circle Club banquet at the 4-H center in Ferndale, thanks to him.

One can walk the hall of fame at the State Fair and see Kiley's name as well as my own, thanks to Sweetie, Precious, Precedence, and Touch of Coal.

The State Fair always ended in the Grooming Contest. Many kids never participated because they were either too tired or didn't have a clue what they were doing. Some kids that showed had the luxury of hiring professional fitters come in the day of shows and get their cattle ready to exhibit. The professionals did everything from bathing and blowing them dry to clipping them and putting adhesive on their legs.

I wanted to take full ownership of my babies, so I always balked at this idea. The Grooming Contest was a chance to show off to the world that I could groom my own cattle, thank you very much. As Shakespeare said, "To thine own self, be true."

Allen Moore and I had won the senior division the year prior. This year, I partnered with Will Sargent. We went through the timed process as a team and did everything required. We washed Shadrach, blew him dry, clipped him, fluffed his leg hair with adhesive, and put his tail in the prettiest ball, hiding the hole between his legs. The contest ended with a mini showmanship.

We stomped the competition. Will and I won the senior division with a whopping 291 points, the second highest being 250. We didn't know it then, but Will and I would win the next year as well, giving me the title three years in a row. Kiley and her partner also won the junior division two years in a row.

We didn't even need the overhead fluorescent lights that day in the barn because Dad's smile lit the whole place up. He was one proud papa. He had instilled hard work into us, and we had both taken ownership of the cow showing experience. Sure, I loved receiving the trophy, cash prize, and bucket of show supplies, but seeing my Dad's grin was the true prize.

After the bulk of showing was done for the week, we were free to explore for a bit on the main strip. The carnival lights were a toy Light Bright, each individual peg creating a menagerie of color against the dark sky.

I rarely rode the carnival rides because words like Tilt-A-Whirl and vomit always went hand in hand with me. Even the sight of the rides turned my stomach into the agitator of a washing machine. I could handle the bumper cars as long as I didn't drive backwards. It was hard to be me, what can I say?

We always went in groups or with our parents since the toothless and dirty carnies scared us so much. The strip was a foreign land, but it beckoned us, like a fruit fly to a rotten peach. People lunged at us from all directions, enticing us to throw a ball into a coke bottle or guess the weight of the fat lady. We weaved our way in and out of screaming children and cigarette smoke to find our destination: the food.

To us, the strip was all about the food. We turned up our noses to the hot dogs, cotton candy, and onion rings and headed straight for the manna from above: giant smoked turkey legs, funnel cakes, and whipped pineapple ice cream cones. It was a special treat after eating the complimentary chicken dinners they provided for exhibitors every evening. The chicken dinners were delicious, but chicken and rice were coming out of our noses by the end of the week. Mom often bypassed the chicken dinners and feasted on Darla Lothes's homemade chili she had so graciously offered. But, as good as her chili was, Mom enjoyed the manna, as well.

Rock music blared our inner eardrums so much we had to yell to hear one another, but we were in food heaven. Bellies full, we meandered back to the barns, where a moo or two welcomed us back to the gift of hearing and the reality of why we had come to the fair.

After the State Fair, I went back home and concentrated on choosing a college. Both the University of Central Arkansas and the University of Arkansas were offering scholarships, but only one was offering a vocal scholarship. If I wanted to sing, then I had to leave home. I was torn.

I had one more year of showing left, so I decided to go big or go home. I threw it all on a steer I named Siete, my 7th and final steer. (I now had a whole new Spanish vocabulary to name animals with, thanks to Mrs. Hinds at Springdale High.) He was my final hope of winning Grand steer at the Arkansas State Fair.

But what started out as a cute and fluffy steer started to gradually look like a bull as the months sped along. I was baffled. What on earth was happening? Dad said the guy we bought him from must have missed a testicle during the castration process. Apparently, one testicle hadn't dropped, but they went ahead with the procedure and didn't disclose the information when we shelled out $3000 for him. Due to Siete's retained testicle, he had the characteristics and actions of a bull. He was a worthless stag.

My dreams of winning state ended early. My final year of showing was just about a bust. My Uncle Jay did his best to redeem the situation by driving up the premium to $1100 of my other steer, Phantom, at the county fair. Phantom brought the most at the sale that year, beating out the Grand Champion and Reserve Champion (which was Kiley's steer, Socks.)

Endings

"There are far far better things ahead
than any we leave behind."
C. S. Lewis

It ended abruptly and all too fast. I had aged
out of showing and the weight of it was as if
Precedence had stepped on my foot, refusing to
move. I was mourning my childhood, the reality of
living in a different town than my family, and the
embarkment on the unknowns of college.

The loss of hope in doing well with my final
steer, Siete, sat heavy on my soul. Defeat was never
how I dreamed of going out. Winning Grand
Champion steer at the Little Rock State Fair was
always my ultimate destination.

I sat on my college dorm room floor at the
University of Central Arkansas in Conway. My rear
was shielded against the cold linoleum with a piece
of carpet Mom and Dad had bought for my room.

My three-thousand-dollar investment
poured into my final steer, Siete, had been a total
wash. It was bitter to leave the show world, having
been lied to, with nothing set right. My other steer,
Phantom, didn't make the sale at Little Rock,
either, and the money I hoped would carry me
through college simply wasn't there.

With all the bravery I could muster, I picked
up the landline phone and dialed a man who lived
hundreds of miles away in small town Iowa. "Mr.
Rocker? This is Becke' Martens. I live in Arkansas."
My voice was quaking stronger than the San
Francisco earthquake of 1906. "I bought a steer
from you last year. The steer was not properly
castrated and he developed into a stag. This was
my final year to show and my dreams of making

67

sale at my state fair were destroyed. I was wondering if you could possibly return my $3000."

I came up for air and almost slammed the phone down, too terrified to wait for his answer.

"Well, um, what did you say your name was?" he asked.

"Becke' Martens, sir." I said.

"Well, Becke', a sale's a sale and I won't be refunding your money," he replied with all the compassion of a murder hornet.

And that was that.

I cried on my dorm floor as Mr. Rocker pounded the final nail into my wooden coffin of cow showing. I didn't understand it then, but God knew that forgiving him would benefit my soul far greater than any refund.

Later that evening, I wiped away the snot, kicked the feed bucket on my dreams, and started studying for my English Literature test. A new season held the weight of beautiful promise, I just didn't know it yet.

Looking back twenty-five years later, I realize the journey never once failed me even though I thought the final destination of winning grand at state did. The journey is always more valuable than one judge's opinion or one seller's refusal to refund money when he botched the castration process.

Every evening before a show, I packed the show box, which was a glorified aluminum tool box. Halter, show stick, combs? Check. Adhesives, tail ties, purple oil? Check. Water hoses, extension cords, clippers? Check. Medicines, grain, buckets? Check.

All those years of showing cattle provided me with my own show box, tools necessary to do life.

When I open up my own show box, I see a huge spray can of persistence that makes me refuse to give up when life gets hard. Learning to laugh at myself through the years sure helped me keep going. Getting back up when I was knocked down (by cow or a person's opinion) helped, too.

The toolbox shows me how to have respect for authority for every person God places me under. I may not have agreed with every decision the judges made in those show rings, but I understood they had earned the right to be there. It was their opinion that counted that day, not mine. Having respect for authority in our days is a lost art, and I am so thankful cow showing helped groom that in me.

I peer again into the toolbox and I see endless days of driving to the barn, washing, blow drying, grooming, feeding, and watering countless cattle. Those days taught me to work hard, even when no one was around to make sure I was doing things correctly. I guess the fancy word for that is integrity. It taught me that most work goes unnoticed and unpraised. I learned there is pleasure to be found in the work itself. Work can truly be its own reward. When God put Adam and Eve in the garden, He gave them work to do even prior to sin messing everything up. Work is a gift; it replaces entitlement with a humble sense of accomplishment.

In the toolbox, I also see sorrow and loss and how to mourn not just animals, but dreams. I learned to rest in God's ways, which would later teach me how to mourn the loss of family members, including Kiley. Cow showing taught me that God is not only the Creator of life but also the One who decides when it is time to pass. I learned to turn my misperceived ownership of my cows back over to the Creator which made the losses more bearable. If I dug deep enough, I could even find purpose behind each pain. God owns the cattle on a thousand hills, including every single one mentioned in these pages. In His lavishness, He gifted me with each cow for a brief time to give me much needed friendship, show me the wonder of birth, fill up our freezer, and bond me with my father. The cattle were God's instruments to use as He desired.

We never really break away from the past. Instead, it becomes the tools we use to build the future. The toolbox provided many things I learned along the way without even knowing it; the lessons would be there when I needed them. All I would have to do was open up the box.

The Smell of Cattle, Hay, and Anticipation

"If the smell of the barn was the first smell
the infant Christ breathed,
then it's good enough for me."
Becke' Martens Stuart

The next twelve years sped by faster than the black Dodge Viper GTS I had my heart set on in high school. I was blessed with a degree in English, a photography business, a loyal husband in Eric Stuart, and son after son.

We didn't own any cattle, but I had been given a million other beautiful things from the Good Father. Still, I longed for the fairgrounds, so I headed that way.

The week was a whirlwind. A mid-week trip to Fayetteville in order to present a trophy in Kiley's memory left my mind tangled up in my teen years, like a fly in a web. Dad, Grandad, Amelia, and I found ourselves at the Washington County Fairgrounds once again. It had been years since I had stepped foot onto the site, and yet, as I walked into the barn, the smell of cattle, hay, and anticipation invaded my nostrils with a 'welcome home.'

The fairgrounds had been home to me for eight years. My first show heifer, Dolly, was sweet to put up with me, since I was a green thing who didn't know the first thing about cattle. About a year in, I finally figured out that a heifer was a female that had never had a calf and that a Hereford was one of the many breeds of beef. Through those eight years, I managed to learn enough to win showmanship awards, state quiz

71

bowls, grooming awards, and grand championships with heifers, bulls, and steers.

The fairgrounds were where God knit my heart deeper with my Dad's. We would unload all of our equipment and cattle, and I knew that it was me and him against the world for those few days. All of our hard work was going to come to fruition. Sure, our whole family was involved, but to me, it was always just me and Dad.

And so, as I inhaled the smell of cattle, hay, and anticipation, the tears started falling. Because coming home sometimes hurts. Because I didn't realize how much I missed it. Because I was just now seeing the importance of how that home had shaped me. Because God didn't allow me to lay my head on that pillow anymore. Because the memories of those days were enough to make me cry, whether it be from the good times or the bad.

As we became mere spectators, I saw myself in the children and teenagers that were exhibiting that night. I was the 11-year-old girl with her hair pulled back tightly who had utter confidence as she stepped into the ring. I was that same girl as her heifer got away and tears rolled down her cheeks not only from the embarrassment, but also from the pain that the chains left as they were yanked out of her hands. I was the teenage boy who started laughing as his heifer started eating his blue sale order slip. I was that same boy that would later allow her to lick my hands, loving the rough texture of her tongue on my skin.

I was the teenage girl who knew it was her year to shine in the steer show. All of the countless hours of trying to grow the steer's hair in the hot summer months would surely pay off this night. All of the countless hours of praying to God to allow a victory would surely be answered. I was the same

72

girl as she smiled when her steer was slapped Grand Champion.

I was the young brunette boy with dimples who talked as country as they come. I chided my friend for not combing my heifer the correct way and then proceeded to tell him how to go about such a fine art. I was the same boy looking at my father, making sure I had her set up correctly. I was the same boy who smiled all over himself when his heifer was named Supreme Champion and took home a trophy bigger than my own frame.

And then, all of a sudden, I was myself. Not the thirty something, but, the thirteen-year-old version of myself standing beside one of the biggest crushes of my showing days. *Now* as grownups with spouses we loved and children we doted on, Eric Walker and I laughed about the good old days, when we apparently held hands for a whole hour at the State Fair and when he slung me over his back, hauling me to the wash rack, soaking me with the water hose.

Showing cattle: the work,   the fair, the joys and the sorrows...you just can't get it unless you've done it. So, as I helped Amelia and Dad present a trophy in memory of Kiley for the Supreme Champion heifer, I thanked God for those days. Days of driving to the barn, washing, grooming, feeding, and showing kept me out of a lot of trouble during my teen years. God gifted me with the very thing needed to put my Dad and me on the same page. God used those days to groom in me a healthy respect for my Dad and an appreciation of his authority in my life. Those days made me one happy heifer.

I will forever be thankful.

P. S. Heaven will smell like cattle, hay, and anticipation that has finally been realized. It will be the smell of coming home.   I'm even betting there will be steak. "Then he sent some more servants and said, 'Tell those who have been invited that I have prepared my dinner: My oxen and fattened cattle have been butchered, and everything is ready. Come to the wedding banquet.'" Matthew 22:4

Acknowledgments

To whom does one owe a childhood? I, like you, was lovingly knit together by the Creator, stamped with His image, and given a purpose. I am thankful He redeemed me at an early age and gave me a song, even in the darkest of nights. He alone delivered me, from Flo-Jo to car accidents, time and time again. It is God who creates, God who saves, and God who delivers.

One of God's greatest gifts is parents. I owe so much to my Dad and Mom. They provided a home of love, nourishment, laughter, and adventure. They taught me the Word of God and practical skills for life. They showered me with grace and discipline, mercy and acceptance.

My childhood was further enriched with the other people God allowed to be part of my story. I can't imagine a childhood without my siblings. Devin, Kiley, Kirby and Amelia were the crayons to my coloring book. My grandparents: Nana, Grandad, Granny, and Pops, taught me so much, whether they knew it or not. Teachers showed up day after day, year after year, faithful to pass on what I needed to succeed. Friends told me I wasn't alone in the world.

Later in life, God gifted me with a writing group. Thank you, Heather Harrison, and Anna Wanamaker, for your constant encouragement. Thank you for reading pieces of my early manuscript and providing thoughtful feedback. You have showed me how to dream.

A special thanks to a teacher who taught two of my kids the beautiful world of grammar. Mendy Clanton, thank you for being my chief editor on this project. I am so grateful for you!

What a treasure my husband is. Thank you, Eric, for encouraging me to pursue this project and hiring a house cleaner so I would have time to write. Thank you for always pushing me into the hard things. You lead us well in the ways of the Lord. God knew you were exactly what I needed! I will always love you.

I am so grateful for my four sons: Cade, Eli, Sam, and Asher. You have filled my heart in ways that you will only understand when you become a parent. You have each shown me God through your loyalty, bravery, strength, wisdom, adventure, joy, grace, and creativity. I hope these snippets of my childhood bless you and give you a few stories to share with your future children.

Finally, to you, dear reader: thanks for giving my story a chance. I hope it spurs you to write down some of your own memories. God's story of *you* is a beautiful one. He is weaving it all together for good.

Made in the USA
Coppell, TX
09 December 2020